Native Peoples of THE SOUTHEAST

By Barbara M. Linde

Gareth Stevens
PUBLISHING

Please visit our website, www.garethstevens.com. For a free color catalog of all our high-quality books, call toll free 1-800-542-2595 or fax 1-877-542-2596.

Library of Congress Cataloging-in-Publication Data

Names: Linde, Barbara M., author.
Title: Native peoples of the Southeast / Barbara M. Linde.
Description: New York : Gareth Stevens Publishing, 2016. | Series: Native peoples of north America | Includes index.
Identifiers: LCCN 2016000749 | ISBN 9781482448283 (pbk.) | ISBN 9781482448184 (library bound) | ISBN 9781482447651 (6 pack)
Subjects: LCSH: Indians of North America–Southern States–Juvenile literature.
Classification: LCC E78.S65 L56 2016 | DDC 975.004/97–dc23
LC record available at http://lccn.loc.gov/2016000749

First Edition

Published in 2017 by
Gareth Stevens Publishing
111 East 14th Street, Suite 349
New York, NY 10003

Copyright © 2017 Gareth Stevens Publishing

Designer: Samantha DeMartin
Editor: Kristen Nelson

Photo credits: Series art AlexTanya/Shutterstock.com; cover, pp. 1, 7, 23 (main) MPI/Archive Photos/Getty Images; p. 5 (main) S. Borisov/Shutterstock.com; p. 5 (map) AlexCovarrubias/Wikimedia Commons; p. 9 (main) Willard R. Culver/National Geographic/Getty Images; p. 9 (inset) Keystone-France/Gamma-Keystone/Getty Images; p. 11 David David Gallery/SuperStock/Getty Images; p. 13 UniversalImagesGroup/Universal Images Group/Getty Images; p. 15 (main) James A. Boardman/Shutterstock.com; p. 15 (inset) Yarnalgo/Wikimedia Commons; p. 17 Phoebe/Wikimedia Commons; p. 19 (top) Science & Society Picture Library/SSPL/Getty Images; p. 19 (bottom) Hulton Archive/Hulton Archive/Getty Images; p. 21 Ebyabe/Wikimedia Commons; p. 23 (map) Bardocz Peter/Shutterstock.com; p. 25 Ed Lallo/The LIFE Images Collection/Getty Images; p. 27 NASA/Getty Images News/Getty Images; p. 28 (Choctaw) Aaron Walden/Wikimedia Commons; p. 29 (Cherokee) courtesy of the Cherokee Nation; p. 29 (Chickasaw) Kotra/Wikimedia Commons.

Printed in the United States of America

CPSIA compliance information: Batch #CS16GS: For further information contact Gareth Stevens, New York, New York at 1-800-542-2595.

CONTENTS

Words in the glossary appear in **bold** type the first time they are used in the text.

The SOUTHEAST

People started living in the southeastern part of North America more than 10,000 years ago. The Southeast **stretches** from the Atlantic Ocean in the east to the Mississippi River in the west. This area includes the land that's now Virginia and Maryland to the north and present-day Florida to the south.

By about 8,000 years ago, some groups of native peoples in the Southeast were settling in villages. The Southeast had many **resources** for native groups living there, including good soil for farming.

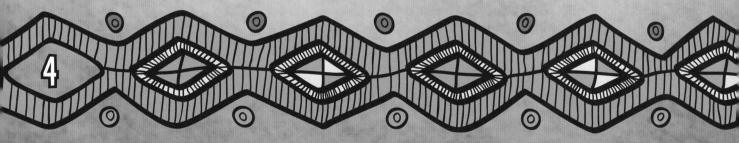

The native peoples of the Southeast and Northeast have sometimes been called Woodland Indians. That's because both **regions** had thick forests. The Southeast also has mountains, rivers, wetlands, and coastal plains.

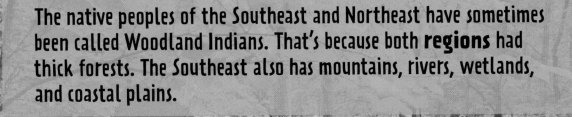

Greenland

Canada

United States

Mexico

█ = where the native peoples of the Southeast lived

TELL ME MORE

The native peoples of the Southeast can be grouped according to the languages they spoke. The largest group spoke Muskogean languages.

Living in the SOUTHEAST

Most native groups in the Southeast lived in villages near a body of water. Large villages had streets and an open space in the center of town for everyone to use. In it, there were large buildings for public gatherings. Around the outside of the village was a tall fence, or palisade, to **protect** the village.

The native peoples of the Southeast belonged to clans, or groups made up of families. One person in each clan belonged to the village **council**. A chief ruled over the whole village.

Public buildings and family homes were built using wood posts, clay, and dried grass.

TELL ME MORE

The native peoples of the Southeast were matrilineal. That means they traced their family history through their mother's family. Most chiefs were men, but there were some female chiefs in the Southeast.

CLOTHING

Native groups in the Southeast commonly wore similar types of clothing, which the women made. Most of the time, they wore deerskin. The men wore a small piece of cloth around their middle called a breechcloth. In cooler weather, they wore long shirts, leggings, and moccasins. Women wore skirts. Sometimes they wore long tops. On really cold days, everyone wore a wrap made of bear or bison fur.

Women and men sometimes wore headbands. Women often added beads to the headbands and other clothing.

Around the year 1900, sewing machines were introduced to native peoples in the Southeast. Seminole women began to make colorful patchwork clothing like this.

DANCING

Dancing was a part of life for all southeastern peoples. Dances celebrated life, death, and marriages. They helped the people get ready for hunting and going to war.

The Stomp Dance was part of the Green Corn **Ceremony**. It took place just before the corn crop was ripe, often in July or August. One person led the dance as men sang and women kept the beat with shell rattles on their legs. Sometimes they danced all night!

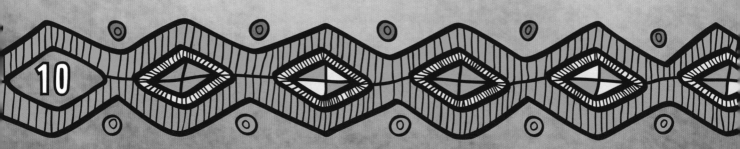

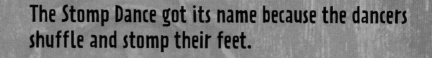
The Stomp Dance got its name because the dancers shuffle and stomp their feet.

TELL ME MORE

During the time of the Green Corn Ceremony, a Cherokee who was fighting with someone would make up with them.

Spiritual BELIEFS

The native peoples of the Southeast had many spiritual beliefs that were alike. They believed in a Great Spirit who created everything. They thought animals, plants, and stones had spirits, or souls. The sun, moon, and natural events like rain and thunder had a spirit, too.

Each village had a shaman, or medicine man. He had a special connection to the spirit world and helped the people make decisions. Sometimes he healed the sick or told the future.

The shaman wore special clothes and masks. He used special words, or chants, to protect people from evil spirits.

TELL ME MORE

The native peoples of the Southeast believed that fire connected them to the Great Spirit, also called the Maker of Breath.

13

The CHOCTAW

The Choctaw lived mostly in present-day Mississippi. They were talented farmers who grew so much corn, pumpkin, and beans, they would trade or sell them.

Games were important to Choctaw **culture**, including stickball, which they've played for hundreds of years. Men played stickball for fun, to settle fights between groups, and to keep in shape for war. It was even called the "little brother of war." A game might have just a few or hundreds of players. The Choctaw word for "stickball" is *ishtaboli*.

The modern game of lacrosse partly came from Native American stickball.

TELL ME MORE

European settlers called the Choctaw, Cherokee, Chickasaw, Creek, and Seminole the "Five **Civilized** Tribes." These groups got along well with Europeans and adopted some of their culture.

The CHICKASAW

The Chickasaw were well-known as great warriors. Some said they were the mightiest warriors of any native people. They fought with other native groups and later the French. Even when outnumbered, the Chickasaw warriors often won.

The Chickasaw men were also excellent hunters. Using bows and arrows, they traveled a long way to catch bison, deer, and other animals. The women were famous for the colorful baskets they **wove**. They also made beautiful pottery and did beadwork on clothes and **jewelry**.

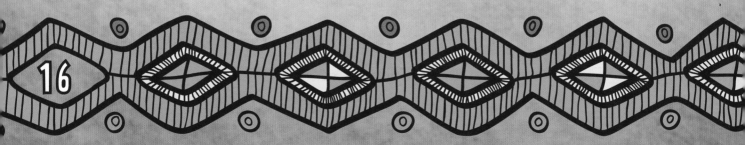

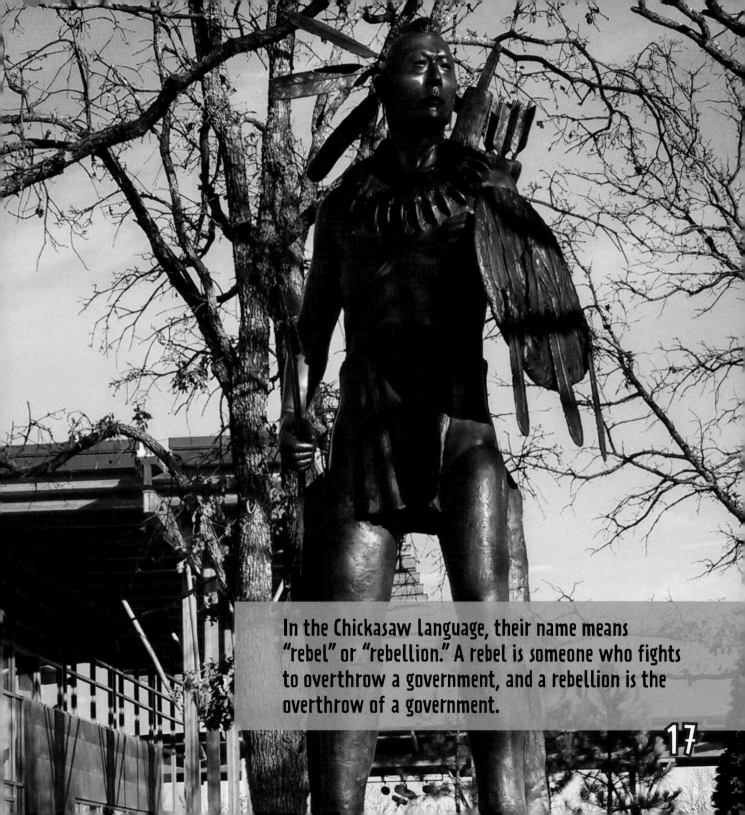

In the Chickasaw language, their name means "rebel" or "rebellion." A rebel is someone who fights to overthrow a government, and a rebellion is the overthrow of a government.

The **CREEK** (Muscogee)

The Creek were a confederacy, or a league of groups that worked together. Their name for themselves was Muscogee. English settlers used the name "Creek" to talk about the native peoples who lived near the Ochese Creek. Then, they began calling all the nearby native groups Creek, too. They were divided into the Upper Creek and Lower Creek, depending on where they lived.

The Creek Confederacy let European **indentured servants** join them. They took in hundreds of African slaves, too.

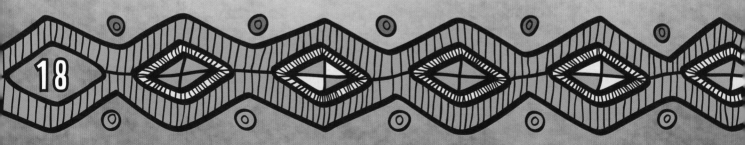

The Creek had special hairstyles. Women often wore their long hair piled on the top of their head. The men shaved the sides of their head.

The Creek lived in the area that makes up Georgia and Alabama today.

19

The SEMINOLE

The Seminole came from native peoples who lived in Florida as long as 12,000 years ago. Many of these early groups died from illnesses brought by the European explorers beginning in the 1500s.

The Seminole made their home in the Everglades. These wetlands were full of alligators, snakes, and other animals. They also flooded easily. So the Seminole built their houses, called chickees, on tall poles about 3 to 4 feet (0.9 to 1.2 m) off the ground.

The Seminole used ladders to climb up to their chickees. The sides of the chickees were open. When it rained, the people used cloth or animal hides as walls.

TELL ME MORE

The native peoples of Florida began to be called "Seminole" by US citizens around the mid-1800s, though there were many independent groups living there.

The CHEROKEE

For a long time, the Cherokee had the same lifestyle and **traditions** as other native peoples of the Southeast. None of them had a written language. In 1821, a Cherokee named Sequoyah created a syllabary, which was a list of symbols, or signs, based on the sounds of the Cherokee language. He began teaching the Cherokee people to read and write.

By 1825, the Cherokee had a printing press. They wrote books in Cherokee. The first national **bilingual** newspaper, the *Cherokee Phoenix*, was published in 1828.

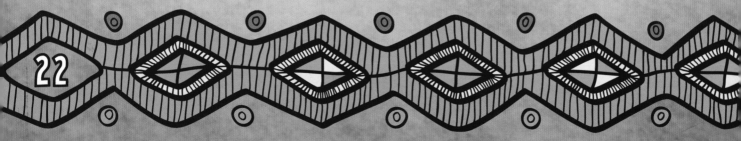

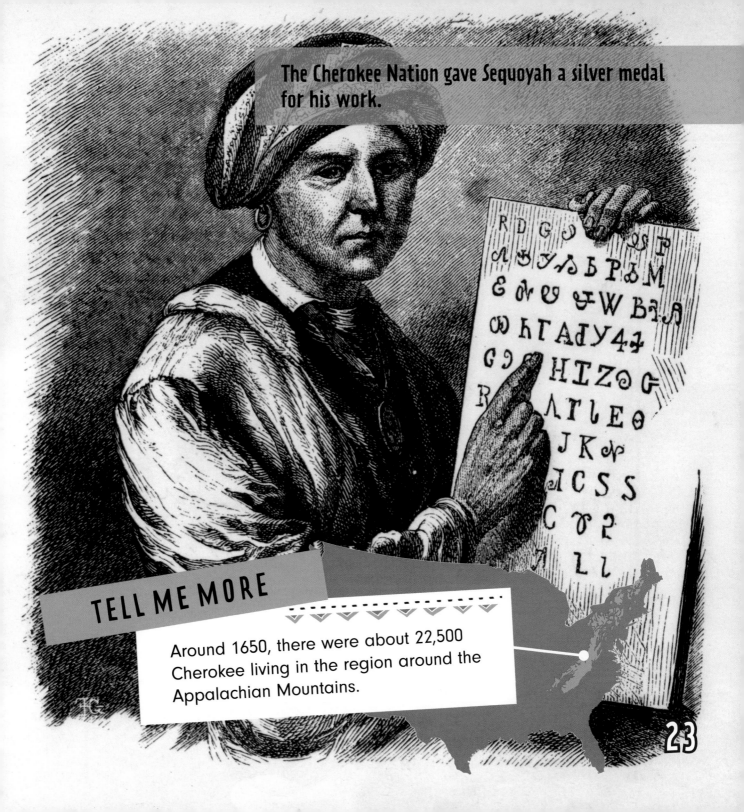

The Cherokee Nation gave Sequoyah a silver medal for his work.

TELL ME MORE

Around 1650, there were about 22,500 Cherokee living in the region around the Appalachian Mountains.

The Trail of TEARS

When European settlers came to the Southeast, they wanted the native peoples' lands. Some of the groups moved west. Others stayed and fought for their land. In 1830, President Andrew Jackson signed the Indian Removal Act, which forced the native peoples off their land.

The Southeast native groups walked over 1,000 miles (1,610 km) west, across the Mississippi River. This move became known as the Trail of Tears. Thousands of people died on the long march.

As many as 100,000 Native Americans traveled the Trail of Tears. They were going to live on land set aside by the government called reservations.

TELL ME MORE

At the time, the western land the native groups were sent to was called "Indian Territory." Now that land is the state of Oklahoma.

Amazing Native AMERICANS

Astronaut John B. Herrington is a member of the Chickasaw Nation. He was the first Native American to go into space. In 2002, he flew on the space shuttle *Endeavour*. Later, he started making a film about the Chickasaw Nation.

Mary G. Ross was a member of the Cherokee Nation. She was the first Native American female engineer. She helped create fighter planes and rockets. After that, she worked on NASA's plans to explore Mars and Venus.

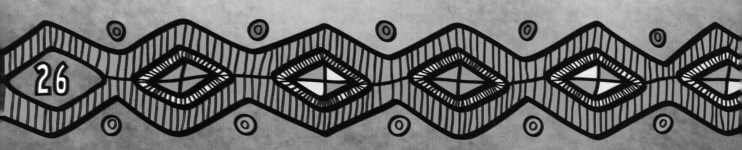

Herrington has spent many years helping the Chickasaw Nation and other Native Americans.

TELL ME MORE

Cynthia Leitich Smith is a member of the Creek (Muscogee) Nation. She writes books for children and young adults. *Indian Shoes* and *Jingle Dancer* are two of her books.

The Great Seals of the
NATIONS

Many Indian nations have a great seal. It shows something about the past of the people.

CHOCTAW The bow without strings and the three arrows show that the people want peace, but will protect themselves.

SEMINOLE A Seminole in a canoe paddles toward a Seminole village.

CHICKASAW The two arrows show that the warrior is watching over the two divisions, or parts, of the tribe.

CREEK (MUSCOGEE) A plow and wheat show that the Muscogee were talented at growing crops.

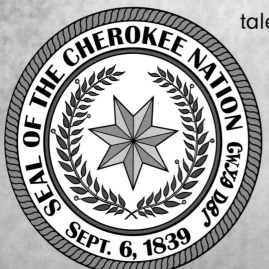

CHEROKEE The words "Cherokee Nation" are written in the syllabary that Sequoyah created.

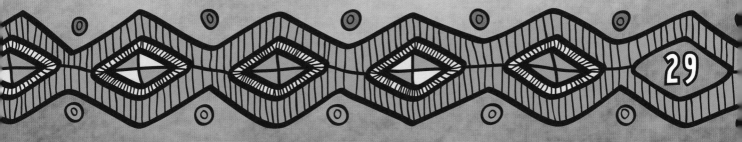

GLOSSARY

bilingual: having to do with two languages

ceremony: an event to honor or celebrate something

civilized: having to do with an organized society with laws

council: a group of people who meet to discuss important issues

culture: the beliefs and ways of life of a group of people

indentured servant: a person who works without pay in return for a free trip to a new country

jewelry: pieces of metal, often holding gems, worn on the body

protect: to keep safe

region: a large area of land that has features that make it different from nearby areas of land

resource: a usable supply of something

stretch: to reach across

tradition: a long-practiced way of doing something

weave: to make baskets or cloth by passing threads or strips of plants over and under in a pattern

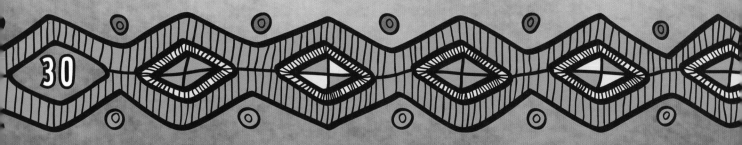

For More INFORMATION

Books

Kuiper, Kathleen, ed. *American Indians of the Northeast and Southeast*. New York, NY: Britannica Educational Publishing, 2012.

Sanford, William R. *Seminole Chief Osceola*. Berkeley Heights, NJ: Enslow Publishers, Inc., 2013.

Websites

National Museum of the American Indian

nmai.si.edu

Learn more about the native peoples of North America through a virtual tour of the museum and links to films and other websites.

Native American Dance Styles

powwows.com/category/articles/powwow/dancing/

Watch videos of Native American powwows and traditional dances.

INDEX